BRILLIANT BODIES

Nails

By Robin Twiddy

KidHaven PUBLISHING

Published in 2023 by
KidHaven Publishing, an Imprint of Greenhaven Publishing, LLC
2544 Clinton St., Buffalo, NY 14224

Written by: Robin Twiddy
Edited by: William Anthony
Designed by: Danielle Rippengill
Image Credits: All images are courtesy of Shutterstock.com, unless otherwise specified. With thanks to Getty Images, Thinkstock Photo and iStockphoto. Front Cover - Talirina, s_maria, Idol Design. 2 - Vladimir Nenezic. 4&5 - Monkey Business Images, marigo20. 6&7 - fizkes, Milena Khosroshvili, Marina Kliets. 8&9 - Africa Studio, DenisProduction.com. 10&11 - kryzhov, Natee K Jindakum, Zapylaiev Kostianty, Vladimir Nenezic. 12&13 - Rawpixel.com, Iryna Dincer. 14&15 - Ozkan Ozmen, aldarinho, Lubava. 16&17 - Josanel Sugasti, Ondrej Prosicky, NataliaVo, Vishnevskiy Vasily. 18&19 - Suntisook.D, Sundays Photography, MZPHOTO.CZ, Kazakov Maksim. 20&21 - siam.pukkato, Jenoche, Roman Samborsky. 22&23 - Sudowoodo.

Cataloging-in-Publication Data

Names: Twiddy, Robin.
Title: Nails / Robin Twiddy.
Description: New York : KidHaven Publishing, 2023. | Series: Brilliant bodies |
Identifiers: ISBN 9781534542945 (pbk.) | ISBN 9781534542969 (library bound) | ISBN 9781534542976 (ebook)
Subjects: LCSH: Fingernails--Juvenile literature. | Nails (Anatomy)--Juvenile literature. | Human physiology--Juvenile literature. | Human body--Juvenile literature.
Classification: LCC QM488.T835 2023 | DDC 612--dc23

Manufactured in the United States of America

CPSIA compliance information: Batch #CWKH23: For further information contact Greenhaven Publishing LLC at 1-844-317-7404.

Please visit our website, www.greenhavenpublishing.com.
For a free color catalog of all our high-quality books, call toll free 1-844-317-7404 or fax 1-844-317-7405.

Find us on

Contents

Bodies Are Brilliant

There are so many different types of bodies. They are all brilliant.

All bodies have brilliant parts. One of those brilliant parts is our nails!

What Are Nails?

If you look at the ends of your fingers and toes, you will find your nails.

Our nails grow from the U-shaped part called the cuticle.

Nails and Hair

Our brilliant nails are made from the same stuff that our hair is made from!

Both hair and nails are made from something called keratin.

Hair and nails both grow very slowly.

Toenails

Toenails are like little shields that keep the ends of our toes safe.

Toenails are flat, hard, and can bend. They are just like the nails on our fingers!

Fingernails

Fingernails are brilliant. They help us do lots of brilliant things.

What do you use your nails for?

Fingernails help us scratch, hold, and pick things up.

Claws or Nails

All monkeys and apes have fingernails and toenails, just like humans.

Many other animals have claws instead of nails. Claws usually have a hook shape.

Animals with Claws

There are lots of different animals with claws.

Sloths use their claws to climb.

Armadillos use their claws to dig for food.

Bears use their claws to catch fish.

The harpy eagle uses its claws to catch small animals.

Dogs use their claws to run and dig.

Tigers use their claws to catch other animals.

Some animals have claws that you may not expect to!

The elephant seal has claws!

The African clawed frog has claws that push out.

Taking Care of Your Nails

It is really important to take care of your nails. Keep them short and clean.

You shouldn't bite your nails. This can be bad for your teeth and the skin around your nails.

Brilliant Bits of Bodies

Bodies are brilliant. Our nails are just one of the brilliant bits of our brilliant bodies.

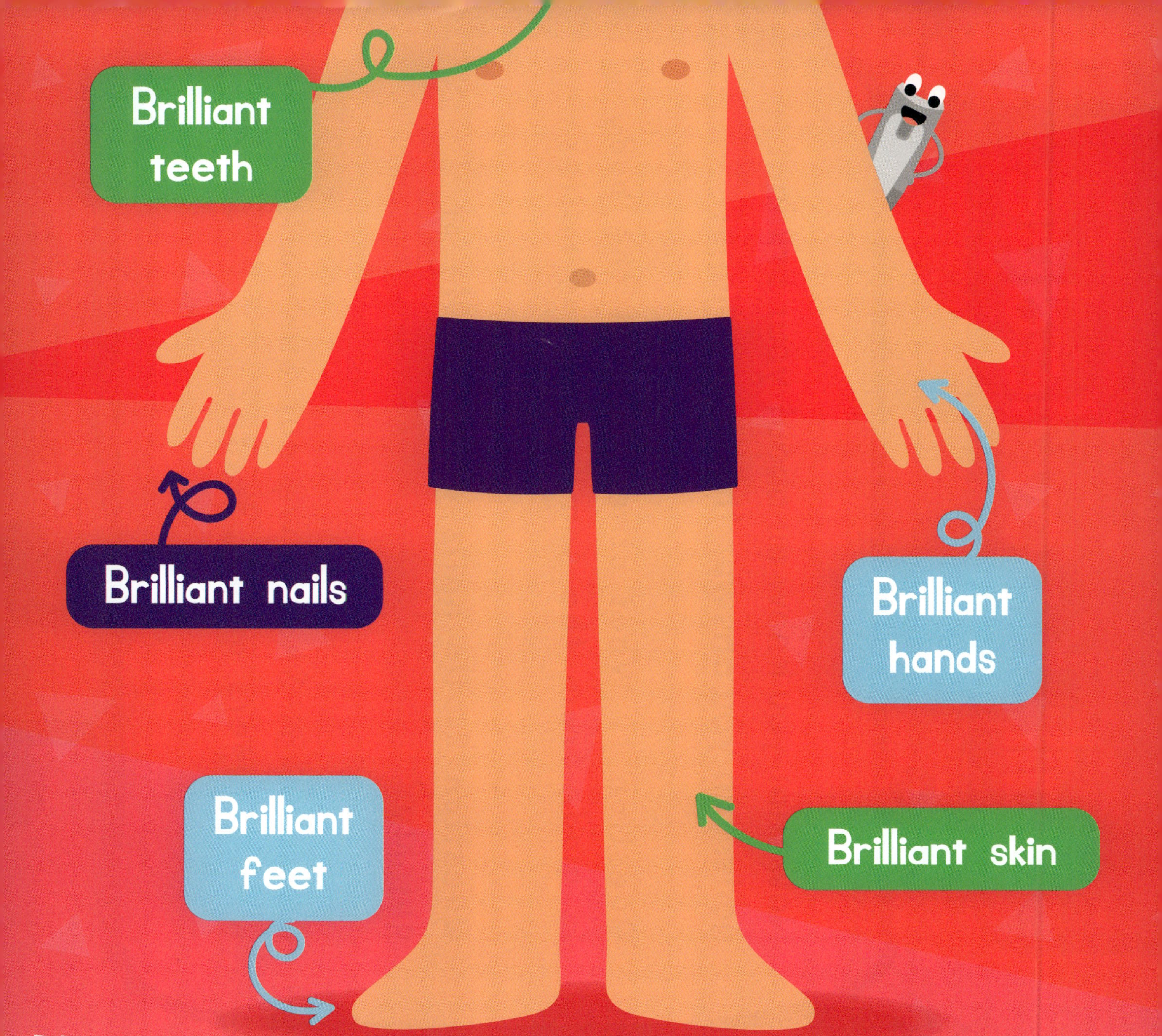
Brilliant teeth
Brilliant nails
Brilliant hands
Brilliant feet
Brilliant skin

Nail Knowledge

Now that you know all about your brilliant nails, can you answer these questions?

Question 1: What other part of the body is made from the same thing as nails?

Question 2: Do nails grow slowly or quickly?

Question 3: Should we cut our nails with clippers or our teeth?

Answers:

Question 1: Hair
Question 2: Slowly
Question 3: Clippers